"Matisse got as
close as one can get
to heaven with a
pair of scissors."

—Romare Bearden

For Maria

BEACH LANE BOOKS
An imprint of Simon & Schuster Children's Publishing Division
1230 Avenue of the Americas, New York, New York 10020
Copyright © 2013 by Jeanette Winter
All rights reserved, including the right of reproduction in whole or in part in any form.
BEACH LANE BOOKS is a trademark of Simon & Schuster, Inc.
For information about special discounts for bulk purchases, please contact Simon & Schuster
Special Sales at 1-866-506-1949 or business@simonandschuster.com.
The Simon & Schuster Speakers Bureau can bring authors to your live event. For more
information or to book an event, contact the Simon & Schuster Speakers Bureau at
1-866-248-3049 or visit our website at www.simonspeakers.com.
Book design by Ann Bobco
The text for this book is set in P22 Stanyan.
The illustrations for this book are rendered in acrylic paint and cut paper.
Manufactured in China
0522 SCP

14 16 18 20 19 17 15
Library of Congress Cataloging-in-Publication Data
Winter, Jeanette.
Henri's scissors / by Jeanette Winter.—1st ed.
p. cm.
ISBN 978-1-4424-6484-1 (hardcover)
ISBN 978-1-4424-6485-8 (eBook)
1. Matisse, Henri, 1869–1954–Juvenile literature. 2. Artists–France–Biography–Juvenile literature.
I. Title.
N6853.M33W56 2013
759.4–dc23
[B]
2012033171

HENRI'S SCISSORS

by jeanette winter

Beach Lane Books

NEW YORK * LONDON * TORONTO * SYDNEY * NEW DELHI

In a small weaving town in France,
a young boy named Henri-Émile-Benoît Matisse
watched his mother paint china.
He wanted to paint too.

He drew pictures in the sand,

and he drew pictures in his schoolbooks.

When Henri was a young man, he drew pictures

in his law books and on contracts, deeds, and wills.

Henri was sick in bed with appendicitis one winter.

His mother gave him a box of paints,
and he painted until he was well.

He kept on painting, forgot about law, and

left his small town to be an artist in Paris.

Henri painted pictures day after day

and year after year.

He was happy, and his paintings made people happy.

But when Matisse was an old man, he fell ill—

so ill he couldn't paint,

so ill he couldn't sit up,

so ill he could only lie in bed and sleep.

His paintings floated by in his dreams.

Matisse finally opened his eyes,
and they were filled with sadness.
Now he must remain in bed
or use a wheelchair.

Would he ever have the energy
to paint again?

When Matisse was strong enough to travel,
he went to the seaside—
the sea air might help him get well.

Before long, he sat up.
A little later, he drew.

Then one day Matisse
picked up a pair of scissors
and cut out shapes
from painted paper—
he was drawing with scissors!

"A pair of scissors
is a wonderful instrument."

Matisse cut paper all day.

"My pleasure
in cutting things out
grows even greater.
Why didn't I think of
it earlier?"

His assistants painted paper for him all day.

"It seems to me that I am
in a second life."

Paper cut-outs covered his walls.

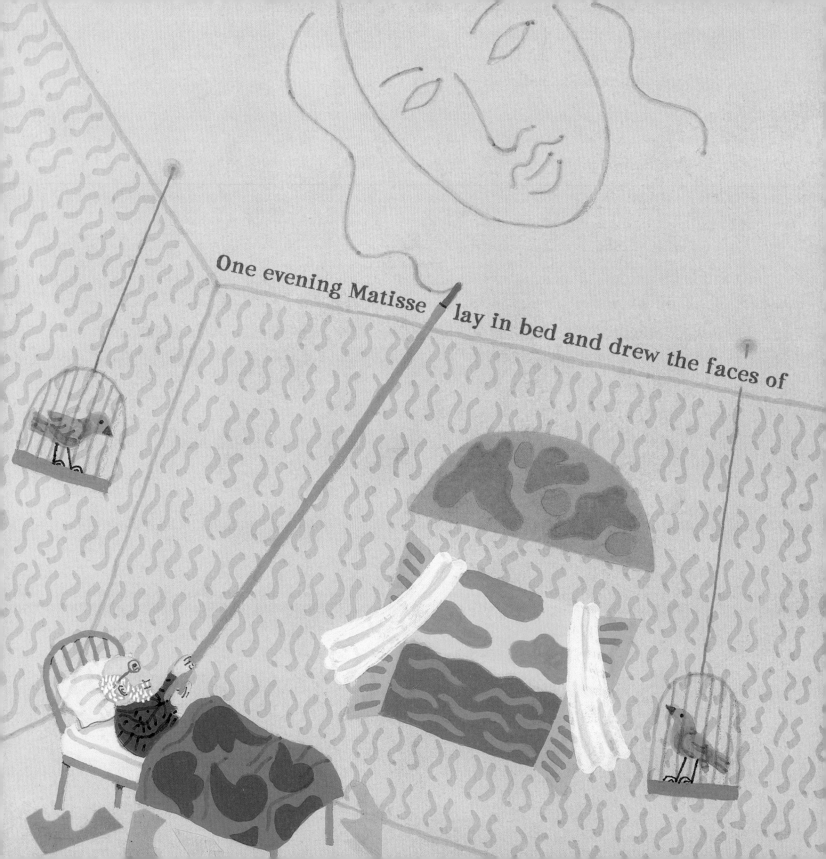

One evening Matisse lay in bed and drew the faces of

As he fell
asleep,
they looked down
on him and saw
his dreams.

his grandchildren on the ceiling with a piece of chalk tied to a long pole.

They saw the SHAPES that surrounded him in sleep.

As time went on, Matisse cut bigger and bigger shapes.
They filled his seaside room with color.

"You see, as I am obliged to remain often in bed . . . I have made a little garden all around me where I can walk. . . . There are leaves, fruits, a bird."

"I am deeply contented, happy."

Then one night, Matisse walked out into his paper garden, and the

rainbow of shapes cradled the old artist and carried him into the heavens.

Are some of the stars
we see at night
coming to us from
Henri's scissors?

Perhaps.

author's note

Henri Matisse was born in Le Cateau-Cambrésis, France, in 1869, and lived most of his life in Paris, where he was in the forefront of avant-garde painting. At age seventy-two, Matisse became seriously ill and survived surgery for cancer. His body was frail, but not his spirit. Matisse began anew with colored paper and a pair of scissors. He died in Nice in 1954.

I had only seen reproductions of Matisse's large cut-outs until I visited the National Gallery in Washington, D.C., in 2001. When I saw the enormous wall-size images there, I felt I was inside Matisse's garden, surrounded by his colors and shapes. That experience was the impetus for this book.

Most helpful to me as I worked were Matisse's own words—especially those from his correspondence with his old friend, writer André Rouveyre, which can be found in MATISSE: A SECOND LIFE (Hazen, 2005).

—J.W.